KNOW
ABOUT
STARS

Mary Gribbin & John Gribbin

What is a star?

A bright star is a huge ball of hot gas, many times bigger than the Earth. It shines because it is hot. The Sun is a star. Other stars don't look as bright as the Sun because they are far away. The nearest star (apart from the Sun) is so far away that light takes more than four years to travel across space to get to us.

Wherever you are in the world, on a clear, cloudless night, away from the glare of the city lights, you will be able to see a sky full of stars. It feels like you are looking at millions of sparkling stars, but actually (even if you are very lucky) you will be able to see no more than a thousand stars.

Cameras attached to telescopes are more sensitive than your eyes. This means that they are able to photograph many more stars than you will ever be able to see with your naked eyes.

3

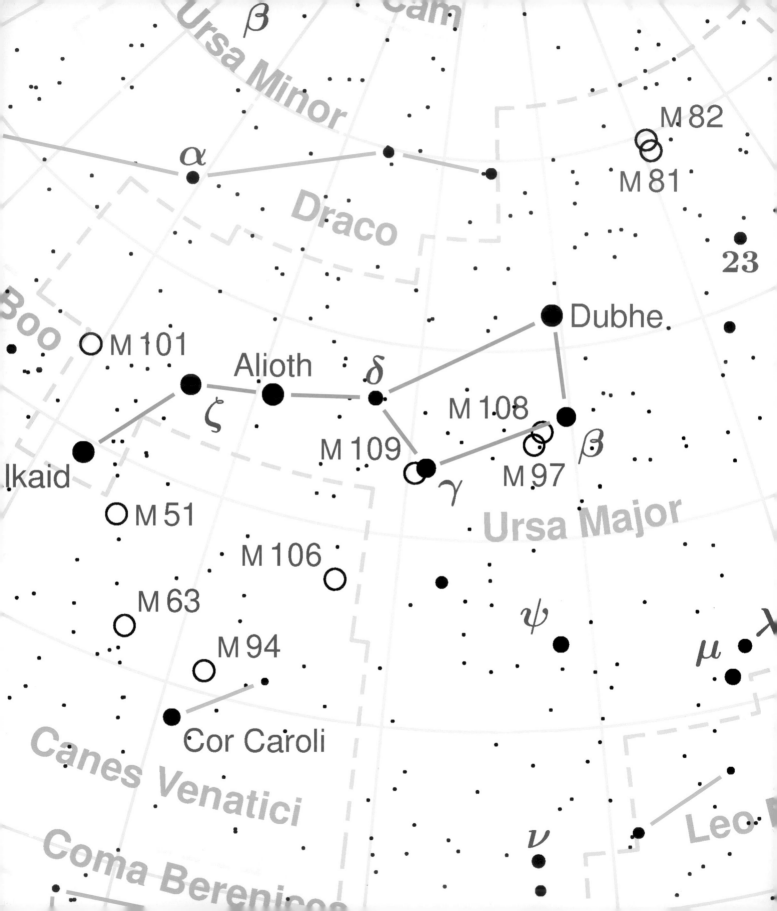

Constellations

Some bright stars make patterns on the sky that create shapes. These shapes are called **constellations**. In the past people didn't know what stars are made of or why they are there. Because the stars seemed so mysterious people made up stories about them, imagining that all the stars they could see were part of different pictures in the sky.

This constellation looks like the outline of an old fashioned plough, or a big saucepan. The two stars at the end of the Plough are called pointers, because they point towards the North Star which is high in the sky over the North Pole. So if you are out in the countryside at night without a compass you can use the Plough and the North Star to find out which way is North.

6

Orion

Long ago people thought that the shape made by these stars was that of a hunter. In the star story Orion is a great hunter, striding like a giant across the sky.

It is a bit like a dot-to-dot picture: join up the stars and you'll reveal the picture. The two stars at the top are his shoulders. The three stars across the middle of Orion look like his belt. The line of stars hanging down from his belt is his mighty sword and the two bright stars underneath his sword represent his knees. One of the stars on Orion's shoulder looks very orange. This is because it is a special kind of star which we will tell you more about on page 14.

If you are in Australia or somewhere else in the Southern Hemisphere, Orion appears upside down! This is because it is really you that is upside down. Your feet are always closer to the middle of the Earth than your head.

The Milky Way

This is a photograph of the **Milky Way**. It is called the Milky Way because it looks as if some milk has been spilt across the night sky. The white 'splash' is the light from millions of stars shining together.

By using powerful telescopes and cameras, astronomers can see that it is made up of millions and millions of stars.

There are about a hundred stars in the Milky Way for every single person alive on Earth today. Can you work out how many stars that is?

Sometimes we see streaks of light across the sky called shooting stars. These are not really stars at all, but tiny bits of dust burning up in the atmosphere of the Earth.

The Sun

Our **Sun** is a star. It looks much brighter than other stars because it is much closer to us. In fact, it is so bright that you should never look directly into it as it could damage your eyes.

In this picture, near the middle of the Sun, there are dark specks called **sun spots**. Each one of these tiny spots is really about as big as the whole of planet Earth.

Earth goes round the Sun once every year. It takes 365 days to go round the Sun once. **Astronomers** describe it as being 'in **orbit**' around the Sun. If the Earth was farther away from the Sun, it would take longer to orbit the Sun.

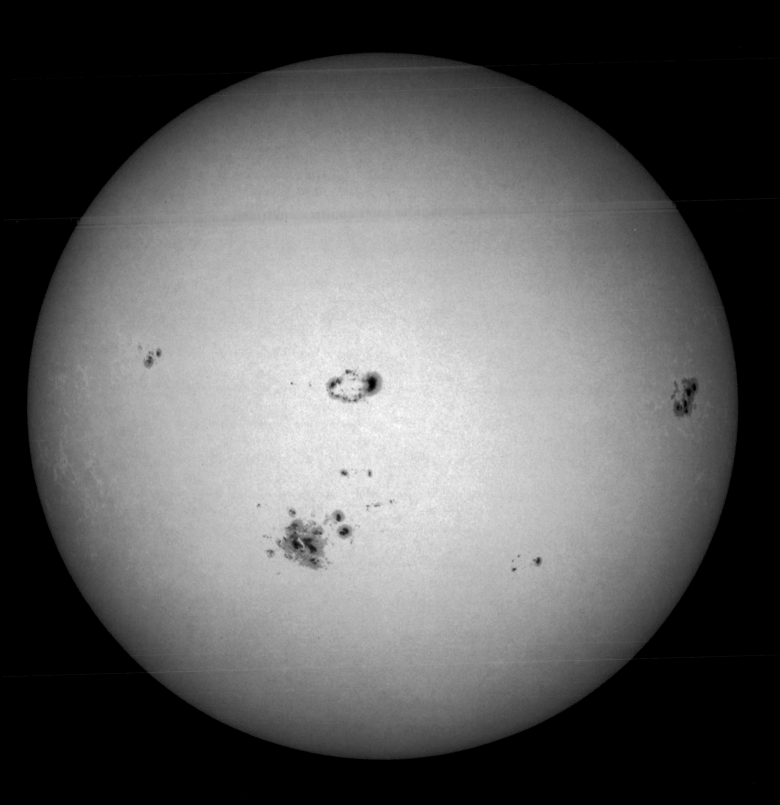

Stars being born

Space isn't just empty. There are clouds of gas and dust that drift through space between the stars.

New stars are made when this gas and dust is blown into clumps. Once a clump forms its weight squashes it into a ball. New stars are constantly born.

This amazing picture was taken by the **Hubble Telescope**, which flies in space above the Earth. You can see where new stars are being made out of a huge cloud of swirling gas between the old stars in the constellation Orion.

This cloud is so far away from us that light takes more than a thousand years to get from the cloud to us, so the cloud is more than a thousand light years away.

A common mistake is to think that a light year is a unit of time — but it isn't! A light year is the distance travelled by light in one year. A light year is a distance of more than 9 thousand billion kilometres (9,460,000,500,000 km).

A Red Giant

Do you recognise this constellation? This time the outline of the mighty hunter, Orion, has been drawn in for you. You can see the bright stars that make up Orion's shoulders, knees, sword and belt.

Can you see the orange spot on Orion's shoulder? This is a giant star called **Betelgeuse**. The name comes from Arabic, and is pronounced 'beetle juice'. Although Betelgeuse is about 500 light years away from us, it can be photographed because its **diameter** is 650 times bigger than the Sun and it radiates 50,000 times as much energy as the Sun. It is the tenth brightest star in the sky. Betelgeuse really is a reddish-orange colour, so it is called a **Red Giant**.

It is so gigantic that if it could be put in the place of our Sun it would swallow up the Earth. It is one of the largest stars known, so it is called a **supergiant**.

Size of Star

Size of Earth's Orbit

Size of Jupiter's Orbit

A White Dwarf

The diameter of the Sun is about a hundred times bigger than that of Earth. But some stars are smaller. These smaller stars are called **white dwarf** stars.

The big bright blob in the middle of the picture is an ordinary sized star called **Sirius**. It is the brightest star in the sky. The white dwarf star is the one that looks like a very small speck of star light in the bottom left corner.

White dwarf stars are made of very dense material. A whole star is packed in to something the size of the Earth. If you could bring a teaspoonful of white dwarf star down to Earth it would weigh as much as an elephant.

The spikes you can see in the picture are not really there. The picture just looks spiky because the bright light has dazzled the camera.

Sirius looks so bright because it is very close to us compared with other stars. It is only 8.6 light years away.

Clusters of Stars

When you look out to space with a telescope you can see that in some places there are thousands and thousands of stars in groups that look as if they are rolled up into a ball. This ball of stars is called a **cluster**. It's a bit like an enormous swarm of bees whirling around in space.

If you get a chance to look at the night sky through a telescope, clusters are some of the prettiest things to see.

This cluster is called M80. It is 28,000 light years away from us. This means that the light which made this picture spent 28,000 years travelling across space before it reached the telescope that took the picture. All the red stars in the picture are giants like Betelgeuse.

19

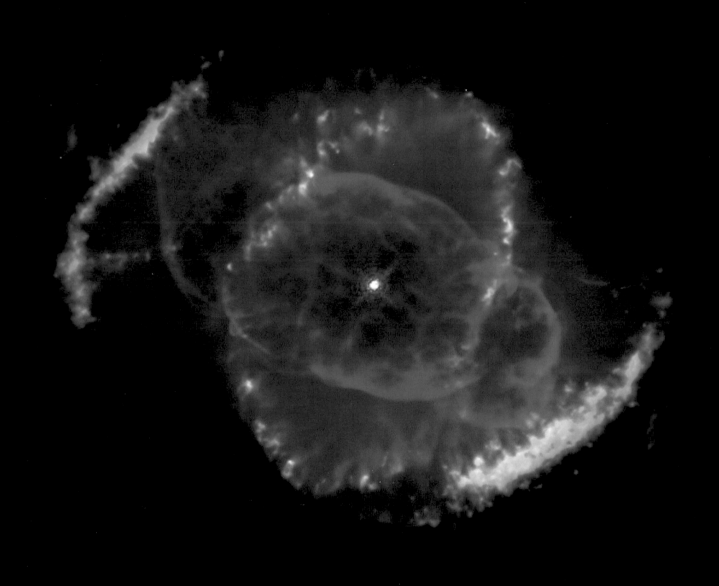

A Dying Star

Stars don't last forever. Some stars live for a few million years, some live for billions of years. Our Sun is nearly 5 billion years old and halfway through its life.

When stars get old they puff out loads and loads of gas, making a beautiful pattern surrounding the star. This is called a **nebula**.

With a telescope and a camera it is possible to take pictures of a nebula. This picture is of a nebula called the Cat's Eye. The little dot in the middle is a star. All the surrounding dust and gas is the old part of the star that has blown away into the surrounding nebula. When all the outer layers of the star have blown away into space, all that is left behind is a tiny white dwarf star.

The word nebula comes from the Greek word for 'cloud'. The word 'nebula' was used because they look like clouds in space. A nebula takes thousands of years to spread out and disperse.

An Exploding Star

Not all stars die quietly. Some blow up in a vast explosion called a **supernova**.

This photo shows how bright a supernova can be. On the left hand side (where the arrow is pointing) you can see there is a little tiny star with hundreds and hundreds of other tiny stars around it. There doesn't seem to be anything special about it at all. But one day it just exploded and became as bright as all the other stars put together.

On the right is a picture of the star when it exploded. When a supernova blows up it throws an enormous amount of stuff out into space. A lot of the gas and dust of the dying star drifts away and eventually helps to make a new star somewhere else.

So just like living things, stars die and are replaced by new stars.

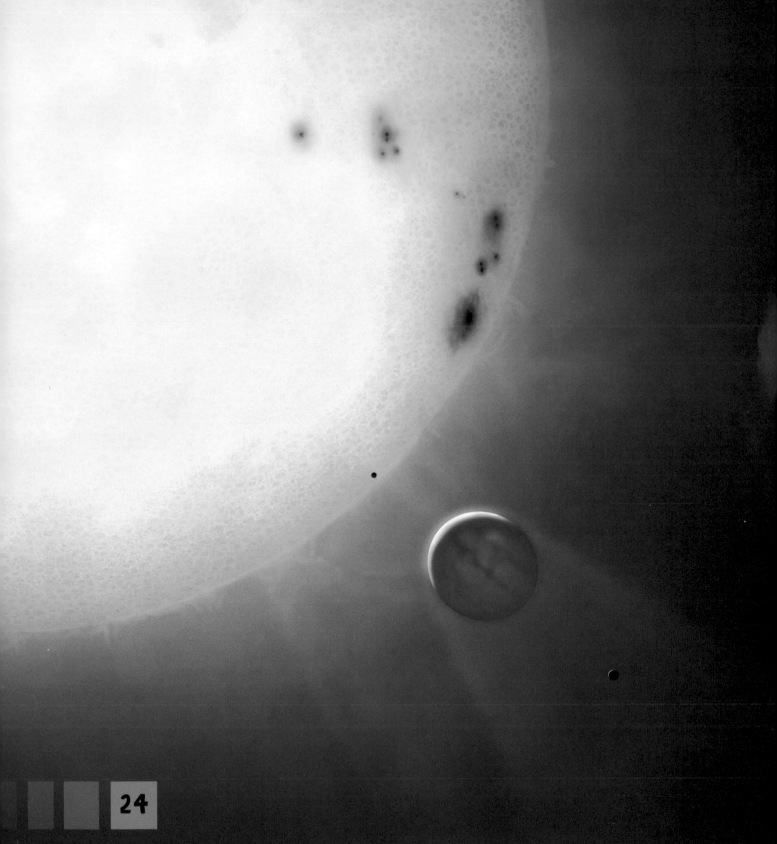

24

When the Sun Dies

When the Sun dies it won't blow up like a supernova. As the sun begins to die it will swell up and turn into a red giant star which will make the Earth so hot that it will burn to a cinder.

This is a painting that shows what happens to a planet like the Earth when its star becomes a red giant.

Eventually the Sun will puff out into a beautiful nebula, shrinking to leave a white dwarf star at the centre. By the time that happens, about half of the material in the Sun will have been blown away into space.

But don't worry. None of this is going to happen for about five billion years!

The Sun was born in a cloud of gas and dust in space about 5 billion years ago. It has another 5 billion years to go before it dies. So it is exactly middle-aged.

A Giant and a Nebula

Just before the Sun shrinks to become a white dwarf, if you could look at it from far, far away this is the sort of thing you might see. It is not a painting but a real photograph.

The photograph is of the Helix Nebula. A cloud of gas is being puffed away from an old red giant star in the middle. Some people think the cloud makes a spiral pattern.

A **helix** is like a spiral staircase, or a fairground helter-skelter slide, which is why the nebula got this name. It could have been called the helter-skelter nebula!

The Helix Nebula is one of the closest to Earth, only about 650 light years away.

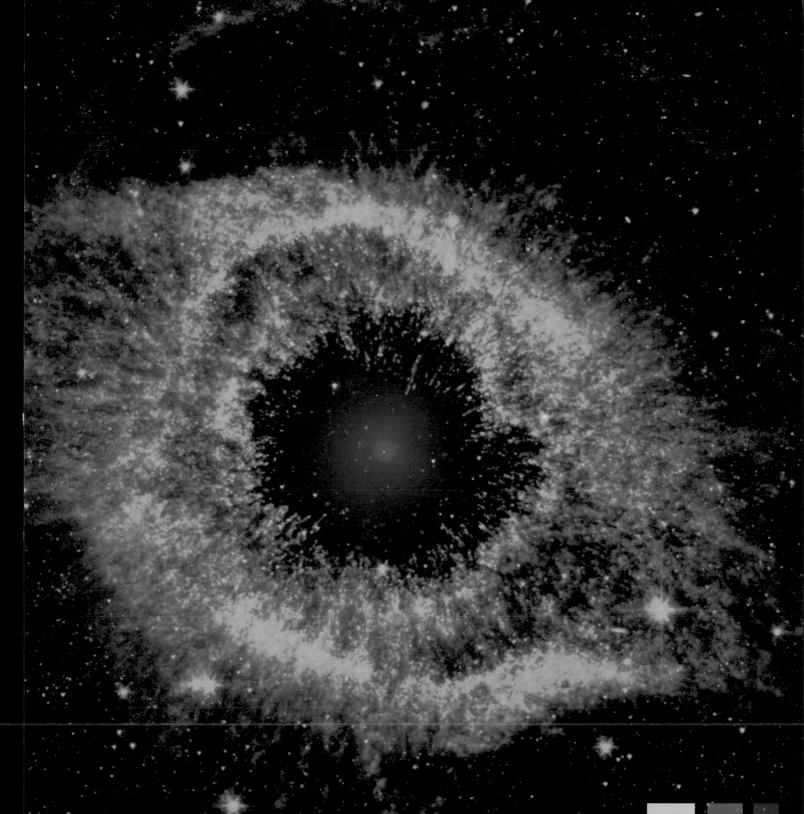

27

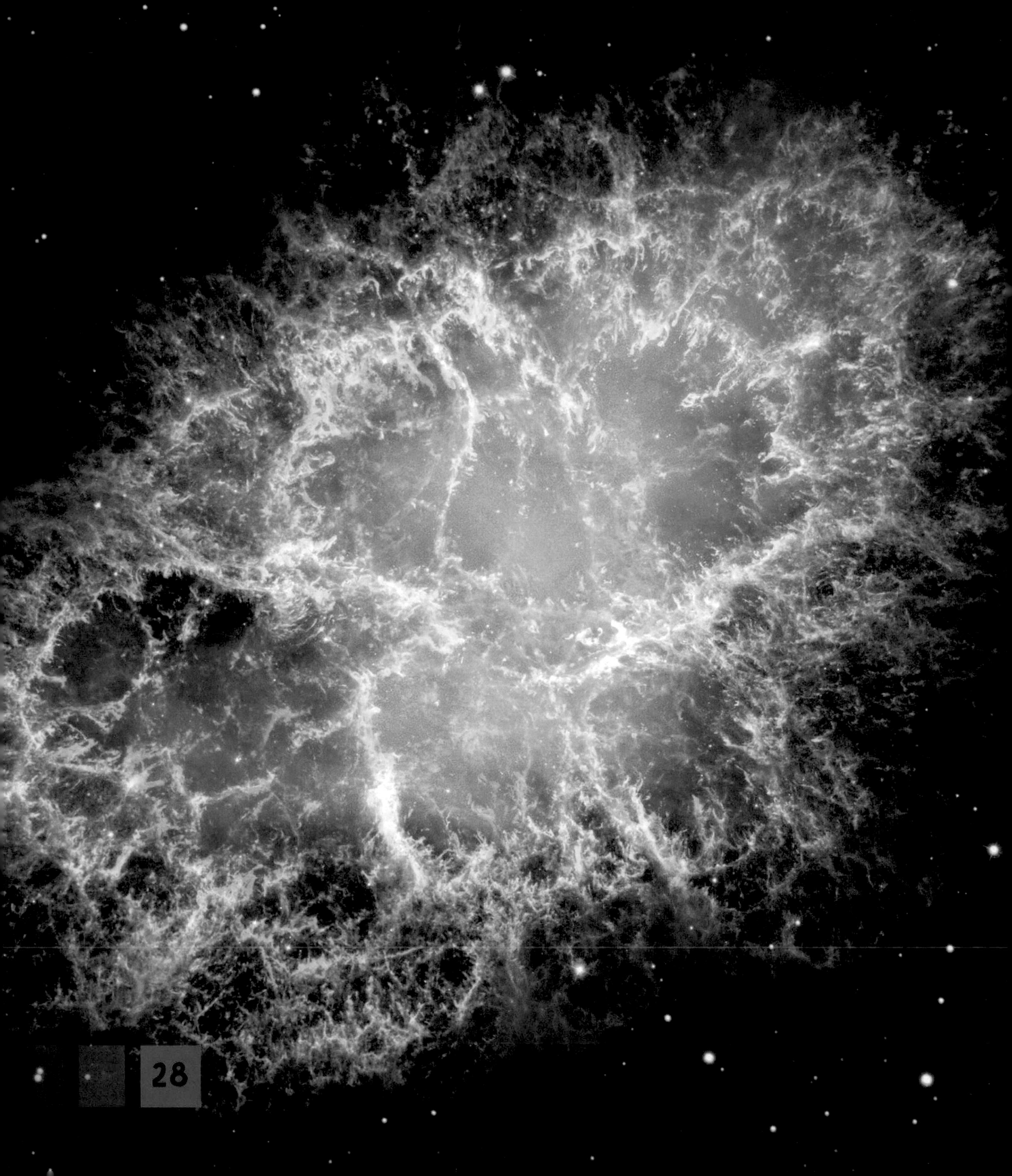

Stardust

When a supernova explodes, it makes a much bigger cloud of gas and dust than a nebula. This is called a **supernova remnant**, because it is the remains of a supernova.

The supernova remnant in this picture is called the Crab. The Crab is the remnant of a supernova that Chinese astronomers saw exploding in the year 1054. It is about 6,500 light years away. It has grown so much that it is now 11 light years across. It is still expanding, at a rate of 1,500 kilometres per second.

This is the kind of stuff that new stars like the Sun, planets like the Earth and even people are made of. We are each made of stardust.

The Hubble Telescope flies in space in orbit around the Earth. It can get good pictures of stars, nebulas and supernova remnants because there is no air in space to interfere with the view. It was launched in 1990 and it is nearly worn out. In the next few years a new space telescope will be sent to replace it.

Glossary

Astronomer
Somebody who studies everything in the Universe, not just stars.

Betelgeuse
A bright orange-red star in the constellation Orion.

Cluster
A group of stars that move together through space, like a swarm of bees.

Constellation
A pattern on the sky made by bright stars.

Diameter
The distance from one side to the other of a circle or a sphere.

Earth
Our home in space. A planet that goes round the Sun once every year.

Helix
A twisting pattern like a spiral staircase.

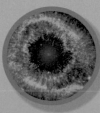

Hemisphere
Half of a sphere, so when we are talking about a hemisphere of Earth, we mean half of the Earth.

Hubble Telescope
A telescope flying in space, in orbit around the Earth. Named after a famous astronomer, Edwin Hubble.

Light year
The distance light travels in a year. Roughly 9,460,000,500,000 km.

Milky Way
A band of white light across the sky made by the light of millions of stars shining together.

Nebula
A cloud of gas and dust in space.

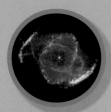

North star
See Pole star.

Orbit
The path followed by a planet as it goes round the Sun, or by a moon as it goes round a planet, or by a satellite like the Hubble telescope as it goes round the Earth.

Orion
A big constellation. In ancient times, people imagined it was the outline of a mighty hunter.

Plough
A constellation.
In ancient times,
people imagined it was
the outline of a plough.
It also looks like a saucepan.

Pole star
A star that would be exactly overhead
if you stood at the North Pole. So if you
can see the Pole star from somewhere
else you know which way is north.

Red giant
A large star, with a
diameter hundreds
of times bigger than
the diameter of the Sun.

Remnant
The remains of anything. A stellar remnant
is the remains of a star.

Sirius
The brightest star in the night sky.

Southern Hemisphere
The half of the Earth that is south of the
equator.

Stardust
A poetical name for all the stuff that
stars throw out into space. We are made
of stardust.

Sun
The nearest star to us. The Sun is an
ordinary star and only looks special
because it is so close.

Sun spots
Dark spots on the
surface of the Sun.

Supergiant
A very large star.

Supernova
The explosive death
of a large star.

Supernova remnant
The remains of a supernova.

White dwarf
The remains of a star like the Sun,
shrunk into a ball the size of the Earth.

For William

The authors thank the Alfred C. Munger Foundation for support.

Photo credits
Akira Fuji/ ESA/Hubble: 6. Christopher J. Picking: 2. David Malin Images © Anglo-Australian Observatory: 23. Mark A.
Garlick (Space-art.co.uk): 24. NASA: SOHO/ESA: 11; ESA/ M. Roberto and the Hubble Space Telescope Orion Treasury Team:
13; A. Dupree (Harvard-Smithsonian CfA), R. Gilland (STSc)/ ESA: 15; ESA/ H. Bond (STScI), and M. Barstow (University of
Leicester): 16; Hubble Heritage Team (Aura/STScI): 19; J.P. Harrington and K.J. Borkowski (University of Maryland): 20; JPL/
Caltech/Univ Arizona: 27; J. Hester (Arizona State University): 28. US National Park Service/ Dan Duriscoe; 7, 8.

A CIP catalogue record for this book is available from the British Library.

First published in the UK in 2009 by the National Maritime Museum, Greenwich, London SE10 9NF
www.nmm.ac.uk/publishing

Text © John and Mary Gribbin

Hardback: 978-1-906367-18-3
Paperback: 978-1-906367-27-5

Printed in China